Student Field Guide
And
Workbook

EthnoQuest™

An Interactive Multimedia Simulation
For Cultural Anthropology Fieldwork
Version 2.0

Frances F. Berdan . Edward A. Stark
Carey Van Loon

©2002 by PEARSON EDUCATION, INC.
Upper Saddle River, New Jersey 07458

ISBN 0-13-097360-2

Printed in the United States of America

ETHNOQUEST

An Ethnographer's Field Guide and Workbook for Assignments 1-6

Preface and Acknowledgments

How to Use this Field Guide and Workbook

PREFACE AND ACKNOWLEDGMENTS

To paraphrase a catchy phrase from <u>Adventures in Fugawiland</u>, EthnoQuest has been years in the making (Price and Gebauer 1996:iii, Mayfield Publishing Company). We began with a germ of an idea in 1996 and have worked together as a team throughout the development and production of this program.

A project of this scope and complexity requires the commitment, confidence, and support of many people beyond the core team. Initial support for the program (both moral and financial) came from Dr. Rowena Santiago, Director of the Teaching Resource Center at California State University at San Bernardino. Support by that center has continued throughout this project, also under the interim direction of Dr. Josephine Mendoza in 1998-99. Early on, as we stumbled around in uncharted territory, it was Dr. Gerard L. Hanley and Jan Boucher of the California State University Long Beach Center for Usability Design in Assessment (CUDA), who steered us in a productive and workable direction. We owe them a strong debt of gratitude for helping us launch this project. CUDA continues to provide us with usability assessment and advice.

Major funding for this project has been provided by a grant from the National Endowment for the Humanities, an independent federal agency (grant # ED-21414-99); we are especially grateful for the very positive support and advice from Judy Jeffery Howard, Jerri Shepherd, and Ralph Canevali of the NEH. Dr. Louis Fernandez, Provost of CSUSB, Dr. John Conley, Dean of the College of Social and Behavioral Sciences at CSUSB, and Michael Ross, Director of Academic Computing and Media, kept the project afloat when we really needed the help. We are truly grateful to them for their strong support, good humor, and generosity. Dr. Fernandez also offered his theatrical

skills as Samuel Pescadero in the program, as did Michael Ross in the role of Ramón

Caballero. The search for funds is an ever-present issue and we appreciate the efforts of

Lisa Jolly of the College of Social and Behavioral Sciences at CSUSB. Also we are

forever appreciative of the good-humored support and ready advice from Stan Stanley of

the CSUSB Foundation.

We also are indebted to Dr. Russell J. Barber and Dr. Peter T. Robertshaw,

successive chairs of the Department of Anthropology at CSUSB. Dr. Barber provided us

with valuable feedback, and Dr. Robertshaw became involved as the irrepressible

Bronislaw Edmund Radcliffe-Pritchard (a name of his coinage). We also received

support from Dr. Julius Kaplan and Dr. Keith Johnson of the CSUSB Office of Graduate

Studies and Faculty Development/Research & Sponsored Programs, and from Dr. Susan

Cooper and Michael Ross, successive Directors of the CSUSB Department of Academic

Computing and Media. Further valuable advice and support were provided by Dr. James

Pierson of the CSUSB Department of Anthropology, Dr. Daniel Whitaker of the CSUSB

Foreign Languages Department, and Dr. Alan Sandstrom of the Indiana University –

Purdue University Fort Wayne Anthropology Department. Dr. Sandstrom also provided

us with some of the background photographs. Additionally we express our appreciation

to Kim Turpin, Director of the Asistencia Mission in Redlands, California, for her

willingness and flexibility in allowing us to photograph at that site. The images on the

sidebar are our creation with the exception of the Wise Man, who is adapted from the

Codex Mendoza (Frances F. Berdan and Patricia Rieff Anawalt, eds. 1992: University of

California Press, volume 4, folio 61r).

We are particularly indebted to Nancy E. Roberts, Publisher at Prentice-Hall. Her enthusiastic and energetic support of this project has been of inestimable value.

Edwin Mercado programmed games 5 and 6, and we are especially grateful for his enthusiastic and timely commitment to this project. We also greatly appreciate the facilitating role played by Steve Shelton.

Several student assistants have been involved with the project. In particular, Alysha Timmons provided valuable technical assistance, and Cristal Cabanillas assisted with the graphics. Edward Caldwell compiled and analyzed usability evaluations that have been of considerable help in identifying and solving hitches before they became recurring problems.

We would also like to thank the many students who have played EthnoQuest in classes conducted by Dr. Frances Berdan at CSUSB and Dr. Robert Tannenbaum at the University of Kentucky. Dr. Tannenbaum's contribution was generous, informed, and thoughtful, and is especially appreciated. The students who played EthnoQuest have freely and creatively critiqued and evaluated EthnoQuest as it has unfolded, and we have incorporated many valuable suggestions from them. We especially thank Marlene Delgado, Martha Cox, and Edward Caldwell for their advice and evaluations.

This program could not have been created without the generosity and, indeed, eagerness, of the cast of Amopan. "Our" characters gave freely of their time and talents to provide EthnoQuest with its special flavor of interactivity. We spent many pleasurable (actually, hilarious) hours in the photographic studio, and enjoyed getting to know each of them better. We are indebted to them for their enthusiasm, spontaneous sense of humor, and belief in us. Here they are:

The Cast of EthnoQuest (in order of appearance):

Airport greeters (alphabetically):

David Alaniz
Jossie Benítez
Sonia Vanessa Casillas
Margo Chavez
Maisie J. Conceicao
Gabriela Guzman
Ramon Holguín
Rosie Jiménez
Trinity Long
Rachel A. Martínez
Joe Payan
Michael Ross, Jr.
Valerie Valadez
Melissa Vásquez
Tony Vilches

In Mexico City:

Pablo Estudiante	Fernando Villapando
Dra. Elsa Sabia	Elsa Valdez
Bronislaw Edmund Radcliffe-Pritchard	Pete Robertshaw

In Amopan:

Juan (child)	Zachary Ross
Eduardo (child)	Jordan Ross
Roberto	Joe Quiroz
Zauhtli	Olivia Rosas
Juan Jefe,	Esteban Díaz
Tochtli León	Davida Villalobos
Padre Raul	Rafael Correa
Sra. Hernández	Olga Morales
Samuel Pescadero	Louis Fernández
Pedro Pescadero	Sam Romero
Juana Mendoza	Maria Lootens
Teodora Curandero	Sylvia Cardenas

Eduardo Jefe	Bernie Moyeda
Juan Milpero	Marv Newman
Gordo	Himself
Luis Curandero	Mike Arredondo
Guadalupe Milpero	Jessica Madison
Pablo Lechuga	Rob García
Tomás Barro	Mayo Toruño

In the Plaza:

Maria Pescadero (Marketday)	Marlene Delgado
Ramón Caballero (A Feud Escalates)	Michael Ross
Feroz (horse)	Sir Archibald Green

To everyone who believed we could do this, thank you.

Frances Berdan
Edward Stark
Carey Van Loon

HOW TO USE THIS FIELD GUIDE AND WORKBOOK

This field guide is intended to assist you in negotiating your way through the EthnoQuest simulations. We recommend that you read through it before entering the village of Amopan, as it should greatly enrich your ethnographic experience.

We have divided this guide into several chapters. This is what they offer you:

Chapter	Theme	Content
1	Introduction to the game	Your project, budget, schedule of research
2	Ethnographic background	Information on the environment, people, and village
3	How to play the game	How to proceed and what to expect; about language use
4	Reminders and hints	The meanings of icons, colors, and the plaza, and how to deal with dialogue, quizzes, fieldnotes and other such matters
5	How to get along in the field	Tips for taking fieldnotes and for a successful fieldwork experience; some useful Nahuatl expressions and terms
6	Extra tips on playing each simulation	Each of the ten simulations' special requirements and expectations
7	Background on ethnographic fieldwork	How to prepare wisely, gain entry, establish your role, select informants, collect meaningful information, and, in general, what to expect and how to cope

The Field Guide concludes with a Glossary and a Bibliography. The glossary offers you a quick reference to essential but somewhat specialized terms that appear in this Field Guide and on the CD-ROM. In the manual, these terms will be in **boldface** type the first time they appear. Following the Glossary is a list of "Some Useful References," should you wish to continue to pursue the fieldwork enterprise or research on Mexican cultures.

The final section consists of a Workbook. The Workbook includes material for you to complete as you undertake your assignments in Amopan. It also provides you with guidance, models, and examples to help you along. Finally, the Workbook contains a Field Notebook which you may use as you take notes.

CHAPTER 1

ABOUT ETHNOQUEST

You are about to enter the world of EthnoQuest. In this interactive role-play adventure, you will assume the identity of a novice **ethnographer** who undertakes cultural anthropological fieldwork in a fictional Mexican village.

EthnoQuest has been designed to answer the knotty question inevitably asked by students in anthropology classes: "What is fieldwork really like?" To answer this question, your instructors may lecture enthusiastically, while sheepishly admitting to embarrassing fieldwork mistakes. They may assign intriguing readings where authors acknowledge blundering about in exotic, even dangerous field situations, ultimately emerging triumphantly with piles and piles of cultural **data**. Or they may orchestrate in-class role-playing or show videos of **anthropologists** working in the field. Helpful as they may be, these strategies usually fall short of furnishing you with a clear sense of the actual excitement, pitfalls, frustrations, triumphs, and constant decision-making involved in ethnographic fieldwork. Since you are looking at life in the field through other peoples' eyes, you probably will still feel distanced from the experience. It remains mysterious and somehow just out of reach.

In the best of all worlds, you may have an opportunity to physically go into the field to conduct original research. But in the absence of an ideal world, EthnoQuest is designed to propel you closer to the fieldwork experience by sending you, in this activity, on a simulated fieldwork adventure to the fictional Mexican village of Amopan. You are a relatively green cultural anthropologist undertaking fieldwork under a grant from the Society for Creative Research. In this version of EthnoQuest you will complete six distinct assignments, including preparing for the field, finding a place to stay, conducting a census, making a map, working in the agricultural fields, making purchases in the marketplace, and learning about Day of the Dead rituals. Future assignments will entail collecting a biography, participating in a village ritual, and becoming involved in local politics and inter-village disputes. Along the way, you must establish and maintain **rapport** with the villagers, learn local customs, and deal with an array of realistic practical problems, social predicaments, and ethical dilemmas.

If you are not planning on pursuing a life of anthropology, EthnoQuest still provides a valuable experience for you. In a general sense, you will be confronted with decision-making and problem-solving situations in a novel cultural setting, experiences readily transferable to a multitude of settings in your own daily life.

Fieldwork (and daily life) is an adventure: demanding, exciting, perplexing, and unpredictable. You will encounter situations with all of these qualities in Amopan. In order to collect your information and complete your assignments, you must establish and maintain good relations with the villagers. You will immerse yourself in village events and customs by becoming a **participant-observer**. Many things will be unfamiliar to you, and you must deal with the unexpected. You will find it very useful to take lots of field notes and to consult the materials stashed in your knapsack. You must also maintain a reasonable level of health in this new setting far from home. Failure to achieve these goals will result in, well, you'll see.

Your Research Proposal

You have submitted a research proposal to the Society for Creative Research explaining the goals of your research and the methods you intend to use. A summary of your full proposal is included here. You will also find this summary in the "Getting There" simulation, and it will be filed in your knapsack for future reference.

UNDERSTANDING LIFE IN A CHANGING BI-ETHNIC COMMUNITY

Summary Research Proposal

The general purpose of my research is to understand the culture of a small bi-ethnic community in a changing world, and to gain insight on how people, with their different personalities and goals, adapt to these dynamic conditions.

More specifically, my research will shed light on traditional and changing customs in the Mexican village of Amopan by studying key aspects of everyday life: community and kinship relations, making a living, interacting in the markets, the education of children, gender relations, marriage customs, political behavior, major ceremonies, and relationships with the world beyond the village. I am especially interested in seeing how these different aspects of life affect one another.

I will obtain information on these customs through interviews, participant-observation, map-making, and the collection of a biography. I will live in Amopan for one year, allowing me to participate in the life of the village for a full annual cycle.

These are your goals for a full year's research. However, in this version of EthnoQuest, you will be responsible for your preliminary preparations and five major assignments ("First Encounters," "Who's Who in Amopan," "Working in the Fields," "Marketday," and "The Day of the Dead")

Your Budget

You have submitted a budget as part of your research proposal. This is obviously important to you, since it provides you with the financial resources to conduct your work in the field. You will also find this budget in "Getting There," and in your knapsack.

Fieldwork Budget

Name: Frances F Berdan

Title: **Understanding Life in a Changing Bi-Ethnic Community**

Budget	**Supplies and Equipment**	US $
	Tape recorder	$250
	150 blank audio tapes	150
	Camera	370
	Film & developing ($12/roll, 100 rolls)	1200
	Polaroid camera	140
	Film for Polaroid camera ($8/roll, 40 rolls)	320
	Video camera	975
	Video tapes ($4 each, 50 tapes)	200
	Lap top computer and diskettes	2900
	Extra batteries	80
	Misc (notebooks, pens, pencils)	100
		6,685
	Transportation	
	Airline Tickets (round trip) to Mexico City	375
	Bus Tickets (round trip) to Amopan	80
		455
	In-field Expenses	
	Local transportation	250
	Lodging expenses **($25 per week)**	1300
	Food **($40 per week)**	2080
	Misc. (e.g. medical, gifts for local exchange)	500
		4130
	Total Field work Budget	**$11,270**

Your Annual Calendar for Research in Amopan

Ultimately, you will be in Amopan for a full year. However, the simulations (or modules) cannot encompass all 365 days (or else you'll never graduate). So the year has been divided into 10 unequal segments, each focusing on a separate assignment. A week of journal entries sets you up for each "field experience." Here is your annual calendar.

ANNUAL CALENDAR FOR RESEARCH IN AMOPAN

Module #	Assignment	Journal Dates	Research Dates	Major Community Events/Activities
1	Getting There	Sept. 3 - Oct. 3	Oct. 5 – June 20	n/a
2	First Encounters	April 1 – June 20	June 21	Fiesta of San Isidro* (and your arrival)
3	Who's Who in Amopan	June 21 – June 27	June 27 – July 14	Plant maize, beans, peanuts, sugar cane
4	Working in the Fields	Aug. 8 – Aug. 14	Aug. 15 – Oct. 10	Aug: harvest beans; Oct: harvest maize, peanuts and plant garbanzos, Independence Day: Sept. 16
5	Marketday	Oct. 16 – Oct. 22	Oct. 23	(maize prices low)
6	The Day of the Dead	Oct. 25 - 29	Oct. 30 – Nov. 2	All Saints: Nov. 1 All Souls: Nov. 2 Revolution Day: Nov. 20*

*Significant events falling outside of the specified journal and research time periods.

CHAPTER 2

ABOUT AMOPAN, ITS PEOPLE, AND ITS ENVIRONS

Amopan (meaning "Nowhere" in **Nahuatl**) is a fictional village set in the remote highlands of eastern Mexico. Much as a novelist might create a "composite character" out of many actual individuals, we have created a "composite village" modeled after many actual villages in the highlands.

You are just below the Tropic of Cancer, and therefore officially in "the tropics." This is a small, contained, mountainous world, on the ragged southern fringe of the long Sierra Madre de Oriental mountain range that extends southward from the Texas border. You are in a region punctuated by steep mountains and gaping **barrancas**, resulting in abrupt and often inconvenient ascents and descents. Travel, therefore, is not always easy; roads must follow the broken topography and often do not take you directly to your chosen destination. The local people make frequent and efficient use of footpaths to travel relatively short distances (usually five miles or less).

In contrast to the drama of topography, rainfall is fairly uniform and quite predictable. Expect a good deal of rain, especially in the summer months. Summer rains often appear as sudden afternoon cloudbursts that swell rivers, then subside within an hour or so. In addition, a steady drizzle known locally as **chipi-chipi** can persistently dampen the region during any month. The small river that passes through Amopan is both a blessing and a curse: it sustains the villagers and their fields in quiet times, wreaks raging havoc in turbulent times. Temperatures are uniformly warm throughout the year, although winter-time winds called **nortes** can send a formidable chill into the region.

You are in a land of semi-tropical forests: pines, cedars, and oaks intermingle with figs, mangos, orchids, and creeping vines.

Amopan is a bi-ethnic, bilingual community with one foot in the past and the other in the modern industrial world. This blending of past and present can be seen in daily life activities, special events, beliefs, personal goals, material culture, and variations in clothing and hairstyles. In a word, the cultural style of the people of Amopan is not only a mixture of two worlds, but also a constantly changing and emerging way of life.

The villagers live mainly off their cultivated fields, producing **maize** (corn), beans, chiles, squash, and a variety of fruits and vegetables. Several also grow sugar cane and coffee for local use and as a cash crop for sale in the market. Most villagers have some turkeys and perhaps a pig or two; a few enterprising villagers raise sheep. Some villagers also fish in the local river or produce goods such as pottery and woven reed mats. Although Amopan has a small population, you will find that its residents display considerable diversity – in social **status**, in **ethnicity**, in occupation, and in personality. You will meet many of these people, and find that each has his or her own special interests, attitudes, biases, and specialized knowledge.

The village itself is laid out along a small river (the Río Amopan) and surrounded by fields and forests. Steep hillsides cradle the community on all sides. One dirt road (that washes out in the rainy season) and several footpaths provide a tenuous link to other villages and towns in the region. Like other villages of comparable size, Amopan has a central **plaza** bounded by the church, community buildings (such as the school and the jail), and commercial establishments (such as the cantina and small store). Individual houses are scattered about nearby. The population is dispersed around the plaza, along the hillsides, and on both sides of the river. Your research efforts will be concentrated in the central area of the village, leaving the eastern side of the river and other outlying areas for another time.

CHAPTER 3

PLAYING ETHNOQUEST: Adventures in Amopan

How to Play EthnoQuest

EthnoQuest consists of a series of mini-simulations, each with its own assignments to complete and its own special problems to overcome. Since your assignments imitate those undertaken by anthropologists in the real world, you will encounter realistic difficulties: some of these are created through your own actions, others are serendipitous and beyond your control. The key for success lies in making wise and informed decisions.

To gain entrance to Amopan, you must sign in with your full name and gender on the introductory screens. You then encounter a screen offering you a choice to undertake "Getting There" (module 1) or to proceed directly to Amopan's main plaza. You should select "Getting There" if this is the first time you have played EthnoQuest or if you wish to review the preliminaries. You may select "Main Plaza" if you are a returning player, and wish to play modules 2-6. This is also a good opportunity to take a look at your sidebar menu. When you run your cursor over the icons, they will light up. Click your mouse to see what is available in each icon. We strongly recommend that you dig through your knapsack, as it is full of useful advice and information.

You are now ready to proceed in EthnoQuest. Just follow the directions on the screen (such as "continue," "enter," "let's go," "ring bell," "view," "try again," and so on). The tips in this field guide (chapters 4 and 6) offer you some specific hints for success. Here are some general things to look for:

- Each mini-simulation proceeds in a similar manner. Journal entries set up each assignment, and also provide you with a capsule review of what has already transpired. The journal pages are followed by a statement of your assignment, and by a specific "To Do List." Be sure to keep your goals in mind as you play each simulation.

- The simulations should be played in order, since fieldwork itself is a cumulative experience, and information and understandings gained in early modules can help you in later ones. Keep this in mind as you play.

- Beyond "Getting There," the simulations confront you with practical problems, social predicaments, and ethical dilemmas. You must solve these problems in the course of completing your assignments.

- You will repeatedly be reminded to take lots of field notes. It's a good idea to do it. This will save you lots of grief at quiz times and at the end of each simulation. Pages for field notes are available in the Workbook at the end of this field guide.

The Simulations of EthnoQuest

You encounter EthnoQuest's first simulation, "Getting There," at the beginning of the program, and find the remaining simulations at the Main Plaza. To play a simulation from the plaza, click on either its number (2-6) or the game's icon (both the number and the icon will light up when you run your cursor over either of them). These are the simulations you will play in this version of EthnoQuest:

THE SIMULATIONS

1. *Getting There*: You make preparations for your fieldwork, including obtaining a grant, packing wisely, and gaining contacts and prior information.

2. *First Encounters*: You establish rapport with the villagers, find a place to stay, and learn some basic information about the village and its inhabitants.

3. *Who's Who in Amopan*: You are introduced to the villagers and their roles as you make a census and update a village map.

4. *Working in the Fields*: You learn about the importance of land, farming tools and technologies, concepts of time, and food categories.

5. *Marketday*: In Amopan's weekly market you map out the selling arrangements, figure out the rules of marketing, and purchase some products.

6. *The Day of the Dead.* You collect ritual and social data on this important domestic ritual by learning about social differences and about the villagers' economic investment in rituals. You also gain insights into relationships between the living and the dead.

While these simulations are designed as a cumulative experience, your instructor may assign them in a particular order to follow course topics. Whatever order you use, be sure to begin with "Getting There" and "First Encounters," since these involve preparing for the field and your initial entrance into the community.

Bronislaw Edmund Radcliffe-Pritchard

You're lucky. A British anthropologist by the name of Bronislaw Edmund Radcliffe-Pritchard conducted fieldwork in the village of Amopan in 1965. Worrying that his notes might mold in the tropical climate, Radcliffe-Pritchard recorded much of his information on 8mm movies and left them in the school library. While somewhat deteriorated, the movies provide you with a glimpse of life in Amopan in the '60s. Importantly, the movies also provide you with an understanding of the problems encountered by this anthropologist in the field – this is very helpful, since you may encounter some of the same difficulties.

The first film is given to you by Profesora Elsa Sabia in "Getting There." Subsequent movies are available in the school library, providing Sra. Hernandez, the schoolteacher, allows you to view them. Better ask first. Movies are stored on shelves, organized by simulation. Once you have played a simulation, the movies of prior simulations are available to you. You may go and watch the movies as often as you wish. Be sure to take notes on what you learn.

How to Interact with the Villagers

Simulations 2 through 6 rely heavily on a continuous dialogue between you and the villagers. Villagers will speak to you through speech bubbles, and you must respond to their questions or statements. At the bottom of the screen you will be given dialogue options: click on your best choice and the villagers will respond to you in turn. Be alert: sometimes you can gain an extra little insight by clicking on a villager's thought bubble. At times unexpected events and problems will interfere with your planned work. Deal with them. You can get help from your knapsack, this field guide, or, if you're lucky, by the intervention of the wise man.

A Note about Language

This version of EthnoQuest is in English. However, the villagers being studied speak either Spanish or Nahuatl, or both. For ease in playing EthnoQuest, Spanish dialogue appears in English; you are considered fluent in Spanish and it is assumed that you respond in that language (even though it appears in English). You will also encounter Nahuatl-speakers, and their dialogue usually will appear in English. These rules apply only to the dialogue. Written material such as signs or letters appear in Spanish or Nahuatl. If you need help, the wise man will help you out, or you can click on an "English" button for a translation.

CHAPTER 4

REMINDERS AND HINTS IN PLAYING ETHNOQUEST

These reminders and hints are here to help you in your journey through

EthnoQuest.

The Icons

The sidebar menu (on the right side of the screen) contains six icons:

1. **EthnoQuest**: When you click on this icon, "About EthnoQuest and

    Credits" will appear on the screen. This contains general information

    on what EthnoQuest is and who has been working behind the scenes to

    make it all happen.

2. **Simulation Title**: When you click on the simulation title (e.g., "Main

    Plaza" or "Who's Who"), a site map will appear to show you your

    location in the overall assignments of EthnoQuest. It lists and

    describes all ten simulations.

3. **Chile Pepper**: The chile pepper scale indicates your current and

    evolving rapport with the villagers as you undertake your fieldwork

    assignments. Every decision you make has a value, and the lighted

    dots on the chile pepper will move up or down depending on your

    success (green dots are positive, red dots are negative).

4. **Knapsack**: You may click on the knapsack icon to access your field

    guide, filed documents, a photo archive you develop, and gifts and

    personal items. Click on the labeled file tabs to open each category.

Items are added to your knapsack as you play and are accessible at any time you wish to refer to them.

5. **Wise Man**: A wise man sits on the sidebar, poised to assist and test you. He serves as a guide as you progress through each assignment, but will also surprise you with pop quizzes and test your understanding of decisions you make.

6. **Footprints**: If you click on the footprints you can quit EthnoQuest or navigate to another location. You may select to stay at your current place in the game, go to the Main Plaza, return to the Welcome page, or exit EthnoQuest entirely. If you choose to exit, you then have the option of saving the game at your last location.

The Plaza

The plaza is the center of the village. From here you enter each of EthnoQuest's assignments (2-6). To proceed to each assignment, click on the appropriate assignment number or icon:

Assignment Number	Title	Icon
2	First Encounters	Two children (Juan and Eduardo Jefe)
3	Who's Who in Amopan	Juan Jefe and Tochtli
4	Working in the Fields	Roberto with spade
5	Marketday	Maria Pescadero with produce
6	The Day of the Dead	Guadalupe Milpero with flowers

You may return to the plaza at any time to replay a game or start a new one. Just click on the footprints and choose "Main Plaza." Select "Welcome" if you wish to go through EthnoQuest from the beginning.

Colors and their Meanings

Certain colors carry meaning. In particular, green means go/good/positive; red means stop/bad/negative.

Dialogue

Throughout EthnoQuest you have conversations with the villagers. You are frequently faced with dialogue options and are required to make decisions between those choices – some are more appropriate than others. You gain feedback on your decisions: good choices encourage cooperation from villagers and yield positive "rapport points"; bad choices result in unpleasant responses and yield negative "rapport points."

Quizzes and Problem-solving Situations

You must respond to the quizzes when the Wise Man asks you. They are "multiple choice" in format; click on your best answer. After you choose, the correct answer appears on the screen. Expect these to become more difficult and varied as you proceed through the simulations.

From time to time you will be faced with inexplicable situations where you must identify the problem facing you, and decide on an avenue for solving the problem. Do so.

Each assignment concludes with a set of questions or a report you must submit to your granting agency. Some questions call for factual information, others require you to think more deeply and apply your analytical and problem solving skills. You need to

16

provide your responses in the old fashioned pencil-and-paper way; forms are included in your workbook.

Field Notes

You should take field notes throughout your stay in Amopan. You will need to enter them in the old fashioned way, with paper and pencil. There is a field notebook at the end of this Field Guide for your use.

Your notes will help you considerably in building an understanding of Amopan's culture. Save them as you proceed through the modules, since information collected in early simulations can be useful to you in later ones.

Access to Additional Information and Clues

EthnoQuest is full of cultural information that can be discovered through a little experimentation.

Be sure to click on **hypertext** (terms bolded and underlined in red), and more details will appear. Click on labeled objects (such as books, paintings, pottery, or baskets). You will find yourself zooming in on many of them and discovering more about them. Take advantage of instructions such as "look inside" and "view."

Be sure to record any information in your field notes that you think may be important. While at first it may be difficult to decide what to record, as you proceed through the modules you will gain more and more confidence in deciding what is important and what is not.

Moving about and Exiting the Game

The footprints on the bottom of the sidebar menu allow you to exit and to move to different parts of the game, as already explained above.

CHAPTER 5

CLUES FOR THE FIELD AND FOR PLAYING ETHNOQUEST

You are not alone in the field. Behind you is a vast fund of experience accumulated by several generations of anthropologists. While you cannot bring them along (except for Bronislaw Edmund Radcliffe-Pritchard), you do have access to their advice, wisdom, and knowledge.

To obtain this assistance, **click** on your knapsack, and then **click** on the orange tab labeled "Field Guide." Here you will find, under "Clues for the Field," some tips for taking good field notes and tips for successful fieldwork in practical, social, and ethical arenas. This same material is included here in your Field Guide.

This information, especially the tips for taking field notes and the guidelines for successful fieldwork, helps you make wise and appropriate decisions. It is therefore a good idea to peruse it **before** you enter Amopan. Feel free to consult this at any time during your stay. Be assured that you will eventually find it absolutely necessary to consult this information.

Some Tips on Taking Good Field Notes

1. Be prepared: have plenty of paper, a flat portable surface, and more than one pen or pencil. If you use a lap-top computer, be sure you have a power source.

2. Include the date and time of day in your notes.

3. Look around you and write down your observations.

4. If you are interviewing, be sure to include information about your informants. This includes *data* (e.g., age, gender, occupation) and *demeanor* (e.g., bored, hurried, curious).

5. Do not take notes unless you know your informants are comfortable about it. You should ask them if it is ok. The same goes for tape recording and photographs.

6. Never let note-taking disrupt the informant's flow (e.g., "Hold on a minute while I get that down...").

7. Be as specific as possible. Write down quotes in the language being spoken.

8. Clearly distinguish fact from impression from interpretation.

9. Only use abbreviations if you can decipher them accurately later.

10. Let the villagers see your notes - don't be secretive about them.

11. Periodically (once a day is good) go over your notes to check for missing data and inviting leads.

12. Be aware of potential harm to your informants if your notes fall into the wrong hands; you may wish to use a code for informants' names.

13. Devise a system of cataloging to enable you to easily retrieve information on specific topics -- be organized.

14. Consider using a tape recorder (if permitted and wise) to reduce your note-taking burden -- this allows you to react and interact better with your informant.

Tips for Successful Fieldwork

Practical Considerations

1. Go through the **appropriate channels** and obtain the **proper permissions** to do your fieldwork. Deliver your permissions to the **appropriate** community leader(s).
2. Recognize that living conditions may be quite different from those at home, and **be flexible** under such different conditions.
3. **Take good care of your health.**
4. Be flexible in your scheduling of activities. Be able to **adjust to new routines** in the field, such as meal schedules and holidays.
5. **Check** and **re-check translations** given you (while maintaining a congenial attitude).
6. **Write up your field notes** as soon as possible, at least by the end of each day of research.
7. **Make periodic assessments** of your progress to see where you are and what you need to do to successfully complete your research. You may wish to involve the local people in these assessments.

Social Considerations

8. **Consider your audience** when you explain your research goals; **don't** talk too much or make overly long and tedious explanations of your research to your informants.
9. **Be patient and relaxed,** and adjust your "personal clock" to that of the community members; take time to "hang out."
10. Be aware that everyone in the community probably **will not trust you** right away. Don't assume that all of them will always be honest and forthcoming with you.
11. Recognize that the **community members may not all get along** splendidly with one another, and that your association with one or another villager may make you suspect in other villagers' eyes.
12. Talk with and obtain information from a **broad sampling of people**, rather than relying on only one or two informants.
13. **Identify "insiders" and "outsiders"** and understand the differences in information that each will offer you.
14. **If you offer gifts, be sure they are appropriate.**
15. **Respect community members' customs and values.**
16. **Respect your informants as individuals**, taking into consideration the many daily-life obligations they have and understanding their priorities (e.g., getting the harvest in, preparing dinner).
17. Realize that **you are not the most important thing** in the villagers' lives.
18. **Let your informants answer** your questions fully (i.e., do not interrupt them) and do not formulate leading questions (e.g., "This is a curing ceremony, isn't it.").
19. **Listen more than you talk.**

20. **View your informants as teachers, and yourself as a learner.**
21. Gracefully **accept invitations** to household or community events.
22. **Participate in expected reciprocities** and **appropriately reward informants** for their time and information (you may offer money, services such as first aid or letter-writing, use of personal property such as your Swiss army knife, or labor as in agricultural work, child care, or house-building).
23. Make an effort to **establish your own identity** among the community members, so they know who you are and can fit you into their scheme of things.
24. "Go with the flow" and **adapt readily to unanticipated and unpredictable events and circumstances.**

Ethical Considerations

25. **Be consistent** in your explanations of why you are there and what you are doing. Do not misrepresent yourself.
26. **Keep commitments and promises.** If you agree to do something or go somewhere, do it.
27. **Maintain appropriate social distance.** Maintain a good balance between participation and observation, and be aware of your **personal involvement** in the villagers' lives.
28. **Respect privileged information** given you, and **do not gossip** to villagers about other villagers. If information has been given to you in trust, violating that trust can result in avoidance and lies, difficulties for the villagers, or worse.
29. If appropriate, serve as an **informal broker** between the local community and outside people and organizations. **Recognize politically sensitive situations.** Be careful in these involvements.
30. Keep in mind your **primary responsibility to the persons you are studying,** and the responsibility to **protect their identities.**
31. Think about the **impact** you are having on the people of the community.

Bonus tip: Remember to call your mother on her birthday.

CHAPTER 6

SOME TIPS FOR PLAYING THE SIMULATIONS

Each simulation presents you with a different assignment, opportunities, and dilemmas. Nonetheless, there are some general strategies that will help you in all of the simulations:

- Keep your assignment clearly in mind at all times.

- Be alert. Look around and observe people, things, and events around you.

- Be thorough. Investigate as many sources of information as you can.

- Be careful not to impose your cultural biases on the villagers, and look out: some villagers may see you as an annoyance or a threat.

- Remember who you are, and what your role is.

- While you are in Amopan to study village life, consider that the villagers are studying you at the same time. Keep in mind that you are under constant scrutiny.

- You set the pace of the game. Take enough time to think about what you're doing.

- Take time to read the journal entries and assignment statement at the beginning of each simulation.

- Keep your field notes up to date.

Getting There

This is the first game you play in EthnoQuest, since it involves preparations for your fieldwork adventure. This mini-game basically serves as your introduction to EthnoQuest. As such, it is the least difficult of the games you will play. Still, you can benefit from the following tips:

- This is your first opportunity to explore the goodies in the sidebar menu. Do it.

- Take time to read your proposal summary, budget, and other preparatory materials. This will help you later on.

- When the opportunity arises, be sure to view the entire video of Bronislaw Edmund Radcliffe-Pritchard. Take notes on what he says.

- This is a good place to begin getting used to clicking on hypertext (terms bolded and underlined in red).

First Encounters

This is the first simulation you play in Amopan itself. Here are a few tips in addition to the general ones:

- Investigate all of your options before making a final decision.

- Learn as much about Amopan as you can by asking questions and looking around.

- Be aware of your surroundings.

- Be alert to the presence of "thought bubbles."

24

- Take into account the differences among villagers you meet. They have different personalities, personal goals, and interests. Some are "insiders" and others are "outsiders."

Who's Who in Amopan

Here are some additional tips to help you work your way through census-taking and map-making:

- Keep in mind that you may be interrupting the villagers' daily activities.

- Some people are friendlier and more accommodating than others. Think about why this may be.

- Think about contradictions or inconsistencies in some of the information you are given, and consider how to resolve those problems.

- Be sure to fill out your census forms completely. Forms are available in your Workbook.

- Consult the sample census form in your knapsack or in your Workbook.

- Don't just look at the maps – study them.

- Consider that the villagers will try to fit you into a category familiar to them.

- Remember that the villagers are just as interested in you as you are in them.

- Think about any practical, social, and ethical problems you encounter.

Working in the Fields

This assignment focuses on fewer villagers than the prior one, and emphasizes a single (though supremely important) activity. You will want to:

- Prepare wisely before heading out to the fields.

- Get to know these villagers better: what they do, what they know, what they value.

- Think about how concepts of time in Amopan affect your behavior.

- By now you have become fairly well established in the village. Consider how your role as an ethnographer relates to your role as a friend.

- Be prepared to view the world of nature from a different perspective.

Marketday

No matter our culture, we tend to have very definite ideas about food. In "Marketday" some of your dearest culinary notions will be challenged. These little tips might help you to succeed in the market and at dinner:

- Attend to your specific chores, but also keep the big picture of the marketplace in mind.

- You will engage in specific marketing behaviors such as bargaining and bartering. Think about the rules behind those behaviors.

- Marketing is not just an economic activity, it's a social one too. Keep in mind how your social relations with various villagers affect your economic interaction with them.

- Be prepared to be offered unfamiliar foods and drinks.

The Day of the Dead

The souls of Amopan's deceased are returning for a feast in their honor. Here are a few tips to help you get into the spirit of the occasion:

- Be aware of the differences between facts and opinions in your discussions with the villagers.

- Continue to take good field notes.

- Think comparatively. You will visit different households and learn about the ritual and its preparations; consider how they are similar and different as you go along.

- Also think about the different social and economic levels you find in this small village.

- Be aware of your changing status and role in the village.

CHAPTER 7

DOING ETHNOGRAPHIC FIELDWORK:

Life in the Field

This section of the manual provides you with a very brief guide to fieldwork fundamentals. In general, the discussion is geared toward research in a village setting.

The Preliminaries

Going into the field requires a great deal of prior thought and preparation. In the first place, you must wisely select an area and a specific place within that area for your investigations. An intelligent and informed selection means that you have considered the political climate of the area (is it accessible?), research already done there (is there an interesting problem for you to solve?), and your own interests (are you truly curious about life in that part of the world?).

You also need to convince a funding agency that your treasured research is indispensable to their goals, thereby obtaining sufficient support for your fieldwork. When you apply for funding you will be required to specify your needs, so you need to consider in advance your travel arrangements, food and lodging while in the field, personal necessities, and equipment (such as tape recorder and camera). You will also need to check if your passport has expired, if you need a visa, and if specific immunizations are required.

One more very important thing -- if at all possible you should try to link into a **network path**, an individual or institution that can ease your entry into your chosen community. If your connections are legitimate and respected by the villagers, your chances of being properly introduced and accepted are greatly increased.

Informed, equipped, and connected, you are now ready to embark on your ethnographic adventure.

Gaining Entry into the Community

If you have had the good fortune (and made the effort) to establish a network path, you will arrive in your chosen community armed with an official letter or perhaps even someone to personally introduce you. Otherwise you enter unannounced, unknown, and perhaps unwelcome.

In either case you need to immediately establish contact with someone in the community who can support you in your endeavors, help you find a place to stay, and in general ease your transition and reduce the trauma of **culture shock**. While very often the first person to greet you will be a child or a non-typical resident (hanging around town while all others are working in field and home), you need to seek out someone with official status.

Keep in mind that your arrival is probably causing something of a stir, and that they are inspecting you every bit as much as you are scrutinizing them.

Establishing Your Role

You are entering the community as a stranger -- no name, no known family, no status, no job. The villagers are likely to be suspicious of you, perhaps accusing you of being a tax collector or a spy. You must do your best to convince them otherwise (unless, of course, you *are* a tax collector or a spy). The rumor will spread rapidly throughout the community.

Whatever you do, do not deceive them as to the purpose of your visit: explain to them in straightforward terms that you are an anthropologist and that you wish to conduct research in their community. This, most likely, will sound odd to them. Depending on the community, the members may have little or no idea what an anthropologist is and does. Your continued stay in the village will do little to dispel them of this mystery: while they are laboring in field and fishery, home and hearth, you are sitting around chatting all day, or measuring things, or appearing at inconvenient moments to ask innumerable pesky questions. To them, you are loafing about, snooping into their private affairs, and persistently asking obvious or dumb questions.

Your work is eased considerably if you establish some kind of role understandable within the context of the community's culture. If you have brought along spouse and/or children, that helps: those roles are surely duplicated within the community. If not, just showing pictures of family members helps the villagers give you a legitimate place in some kinship network -- it reduces your "oddness."

While you will be engaging in participant-observation, you must accept the fact that you will always be an "outsider." You may be adopted into your chosen group or given an established position within the community, but you still will be perceived as "different" by the villagers. You walk a tightrope: on the one hand being an outsider and looking from the outside in to maintain objectivity; on the other, participating enough as an "insider" to gain sensitive insights into the society's most subtle norms and values.

Achieving Rapport and Maintaining Objectivity

The duration of your stay will vary from project to project, but in any case you must establish and maintain good rapport with the villagers. Your work depends on their generosity and good will, and you must make every effort to maintain good interpersonal relations. You must do this even if you are faced with hostility from some villagers -- you must be prepared for the possibility that while you think yourself quite likable, some villagers may find you detestable and threatening. On the other hand, you will probably gain life-long friends among other villagers. And you must be cautious of those who would like to take advantage of you -- demanding material things or special favors.

Even in the smallest community you will encounter a delicious variety of personalities. Establishing and maintaining rapport with as many of these individuals as possible is a difficult goal (it's surely hard enough at home), but it should be high on your list of fieldwork priorities. A key word here is flexibility.

Living for a considerable amount of time with these individuals will tend to interfere with your objectivity. Your scientific goals will be constantly competing with your humanistic ones.

Selecting and Rewarding Informants

From your first day in the field you will be aware of variation among community members. Even in the smallest villages, there are subtle and not-so-subtle differences in political position, social standing, economic well-being, knowledge, and personalities among the inhabitants. Obviously you are interested in obtaining as accurate and realistic information about the culture as possible. You therefore need to select informants that are both willing and knowledgeable about the areas you are studying. If, for instance, you are concentrating on farming practices, you will spend considerable time with farmers; if cooking is your focus, you need to relate to a housewife; and curing questions would lead you to the local shaman or midwife. Sometimes you wish to learn about broad issues affecting the village and seek a range of opinions. In those cases, it is good to cast as wide a net as possible. And don't forget that children frequently tell you things that adults would not (something you have probably experienced in your own culture).

Often the informants select you as much as you select them. Some individuals may be more curious about you, have a bit more time on their hands, or see some advantage in getting to know you better. You may encounter someone who follows you about (whether you wish it or not), answering questions you pose to other individuals. Good luck. (Actually, other villagers typically don't appreciate this either, and will take care of the situation for you.)

Your ethnographic activities may not be perceived as useful to (or even welcomed by) the members of the community. After all, aside from offering some amusement as you stumble through the language and culture, you may be viewed as something of a pest. You therefore must find some appropriate way of compensating and rewarding the individuals who help you. Expressions of your friendship are always welcome, and can be translated into social and economic terms: helping with the harvest, joining in making massive quantities of tamales for a special occasion, serving as a godparent, doing an errand--that sort of thing. These are contained within the villagers' known cultural arena: they enhance your rapport, help to integrate you into the daily life of the community, and also offer you insights into these activities. Another avenue is to be generous with your photography--a Polaroid camera is extremely helpful in instantly providing individuals with their own pictures, which are typically valued very highly.

Since you are probably used to paying for services rendered, you may be tempted to do so here. Virtually all villagers today are involved in a monetized economy to some degree or other. You will often find it agreeable to purchase pottery from the potter, clothing from the weaver, and herbs from the midwife, even if you don't really need them.

How to Obtain, Evaluate, Record and Organize Information

You are in the field to collect **data** on a specific culture. Sometimes this data is then amassed and systematized to create a thorough, general description, or ethnography of the culture. Other times this data is presented as **evidence** for a specific scholarly argument, such as debating the nature of interpersonal relations in small communities, or resolving the role of ritual (or economy, or politics) in driving culture change. Both goals are important: the first adds to the fund of cultural knowledge world-wide, the second contributes to our understanding of how cultures work, interact, and change.

Anthropologists collect cultural data primarily through **participant-observation**, map-making, structured interviews as in census-taking, open-ended interviews, and in-depth interviews.

Most of what anthropologists do in the field is called participant-observation. This involves exposure to and engagement in the everyday activities of the individuals being studied. Participating in ordinary and extraordinary activities means, quite obviously, that the ethnographer must gain positive rapport with members of the community, and must "get out there." Observation requires that you be alert to the setting, people, and activities around you.

Much in culture is subtle and goes unmentioned or even unrecognized by those participating in the culture. Participant-observation allows the ethnographer to gain access to those subtleties by being immersed in day-to-day routines, and by having to cope with relationships and events in a comfortable, customary manner. Typically your new friends will let you know when you have not caught on. Sometimes, out of politeness, they may not, and you may plod along for some time in a morass of misunderstandings.

When you first arrive in your field situation, much of what you observe will be driven by necessity--you may be trying, for instance, to locate a key contact or find a place to stay. In such cases, you will tend to direct your observations accordingly: if seeking a person, you will focus on individuals; if seeking a place, you will observe buildings or landmarks. Depending on your research goals, you will probably identify and concentrate on specific settings for your participation and observations. You would be likely to spend a great deal of time in homes for a study of child-rearing practices, in the public square for a study of social interaction, in the market for an investigation of economic exchange patterns, and in the local cantina or pub for a look into drinking habits. It is logical to choose your settings appropriately, while also being prepared to enter other settings if they apply to your study.

Making a map, or series of maps, is essential to your understanding of the community and should be undertaken early in your stay. It is sometimes useful to employ one or more community members in this activity.

Structured interviews are a useful technique in another early activity: compiling a census of community members. The census records at least their household and kinship relations, age, gender, marital status, occupation, and language(s) spoken. For these structured interviews it is convenient to have a prepared form at your disposal. Be careful, however, not to become a slave to the form and hence miss some interesting cultural tidbits offered by your informants.

Structured interviews provide you with specific cultural information that you expect to find, at least in a general sense. But there is a tendency to structure these interviews according to your own, or anticipated, cultural categories. Open-ended interviews give more freedom of expression to your informants. You can approach such interviews by asking general or specific information questions, and allowing your informants to hold forth. You may also solicit opinions, again giving your informants an opportunity for uninterrupted discourse.

In-depth interviews are especially useful in obtaining information on an individual's life history, occupational or other focused activities, or specialized knowledge. It is important to choose an appropriate informant for the information you seek, and to select a time and place with few expected interruptions. Since this requires considerable time from your informants, be considerate of their time constraints, and also be aware of their attention span. If they get bored or impatient, continue at another time.

As you use these various methods of obtaining information, you should be constantly evaluating its veracity. Consider if your informant is the best qualified person to provide the information sought: a housewife for cooking techniques, a farmer for agricultural knowledge, the midwife for herbal remedies, or the presidente for local politics. While these individuals are fonts of specialized knowledge, you should keep in mind that they also have their specific points of view and biases. It is typically a good idea to reaffirm information you collect.

You must also record your data in a thorough and systematic manner. You may use a laptop computer (if electricity is available), tape recorder, and traditional pen and paper. For tips on taking effective field notes, check chapter 5 in this manual, or the field guide section in your CD-ROM knapsack.

Practical Considerations

Too hot. Too cold. Too windy. Too many bugs. Creepy snakes. Suspicious-looking food. That sick feeling. Uncomfortable beds (or ground). Roads washed out. No privacy. No electricity, bathrooms, or running water.

Conditions in the field may be quite different from what you are accustomed to, and you may find yourself uncomfortable (physically and mentally) for a while. But to conduct successful fieldwork, you must adapt to these new conditions without complaint.

You can do it. Keep in mind that those chubby black fried ants you have just been offered may be considered an expensive delicacy.

A primary practical consideration in the field is maintaining your health. A different environment, diet, and schedule all conspire to place stresses on your physical well-being. Come prepared with essential medicines and a first aid kit. Know where the nearest clinic is located, but be advised that the local shaman or midwife may insist on their cures as more potent. Be prepared to make a decision about this sort of thing.

Ethical Considerations

You enter the field with your own collection of ideas, beliefs, and standards. They are part of your background and traditions. Yet now you are living under an entirely (or almost entirely) different set of rules. Some of the problems you face will be straightforward, and their solutions relatively easy and non-controversial. Others will be baffling and perhaps confront you with perplexing moral dilemmas. This is the realm of the ethical.

While each field situation is unique, there are certain ethical considerations that anthropologists frequently face. Here's a sampling:

- Maintaining your primary responsibility to the persons you are studying, and protecting their identities. This must be balanced with your ability to present an accurate picture of the community's cultural and social life.

- Obtaining clear consent from informants for collecting information, some of which may be sensitive. Are you sure they understand what you are doing?

- Playing a part in the increasing dependence of the community members on outside forces, such as commodities, services, and ideas. What kind of a role do you play?

- Keeping in mind your responsibility to contribute in some appropriate way to the people you are studying, and the effects that may have on them.

- Offering medical services. There are likely to be many situations where your role as a human being overshadows your role as a researcher, and you are asked to give aid. In doing so, you may run into conflicts with a local curer, or you may become so popular that people become dependent on your services.

- Being asked for advice on sensitive and complicated issues. You may be asked to offer a political opinion, to intervene in an interpersonal problem, to help one person at the expense of others, or to serve as an intermediary for the community.

- Keeping promises. This can be tricky, especially if you made a promise based on incomplete or inaccurate information, and now feel that the best course of action is to back out even though you have already established the expectations.

Ethical problems such as these (and a myriad of others) have no easy solutions.

Typically, a solution will yield some positive consequences (such as offering a cure in an emergency) and some negative ones (such as alienating the local curer).

Exiting the Field

It's time to leave. Your grant money is spent, your family and friends miss you, and you need a shower. If you are like most ethnographers, you are pleased with the amount of data you have amassed, and happy with the new friends you have made. But also like many ethnographers, you feel like you have only touched the surface of cultural understanding. You may even arrive at your most astounding insights on the day before your departure.

Much ethnographic field research is a continuous endeavor, with ethnographers returning to their research sites over a period of many years. There is a great benefit to this: community members come to trust you the better they know you, and will tend to reveal cultural details and subtleties that would otherwise be denied you. You also learn to ask more productive and more culturally appropriate questions. The result should be a solid and sensitive ethnographic study. And, don't forget to stay in touch with those individuals who have been so generous and friendly to you.

Remember the culture shock you felt upon entering the field? After a year or so in that cultural setting, you now must return to your own culture. You are likely to experience culture shock once again, but in reverse. While you may find it difficult, it is nonetheless a priceless learning experience.

GLOSSARY

Aguardiente: An alcoholic beverage made from sugar cane.

Amaranth: A plant yielding small seeds that are ground and made into a dough.

Amate: Native paper manufactured from the inner bark of a fig tree.

Amopan: A fictional community set in a mountainous area of eastern Mexico.

Anthropologist: A person who studies human beings and their diverse cultures.

Atole: A hot non-alcoholic beverage usually made from maize gruel, but occasionally from rice, squash, or sweet potatoes. Sometimes the gruel is lightly fermented.

Backstrap Loom: A hand loom consisting of, essentially, a bundle of sticks to which are attached threads for weaving cloth; one end of the loom is attached to a post while the other end wraps around the weaver's back.

Bargaining: Haggling over a price to arrive at an agreement between buyer and seller.

Barranca: A steep, deep gorge.

Barter: Exchanging goods for goods; services may also be exchanged through barter.

Biblioteca: Library.

Cacique: A "political boss" who runs the political affairs of the community from behind the scenes.

Caldo: A soup or stew. Caldo la Sorpresa is "Surprise Soup."

Cantina: A combination bar and café, and often a center of community life, especially for men.

Case study: A detailed account of a single, notable incident or event.

Casuela: A large ceramic casserole dish used for cooking and serving food.

Census: A detailed account of all the inhabitants of a community; should include name, household residence, gender, age, occupation, and relationships to others in the community.

Chipi-chipi: A slow, relentless drizzle.

Coa: A hand-held hoe used for cultivating and weeding.

Comalli: A broad, round pottery griddle used mainly for cooking tortillas.

Compadrazgo: The institution of godparenthood, most commonly involving the sponsorship of infants at baptism by a couple chosen by the infant's parents. Creates strong bonds between the pairs of adults. See **padrino** and **madrina**.

Copal: A resin from copal trees; burned as incense.

Culture: Learned rules, beliefs, and behaviors shared by a particular group of people.

Culture shock: Trauma faced by the ethnographer in the early stages of fieldwork.

Data: The raw, detailed information from which an ethnographic picture of a society and culture can be derived.

Day of the Dead: An annual ceremony celebrated November 1 and 2 in honor of the recently departed. See **Todos Santos**.

Elote worms: Worms that feed on the young corn cobs in the fields.

Ethics: A moral code that defines the ethnographer's responsibilities and proprieties.

Ethnicity: Association with a particular cultural group.

Ethnocentrism: Viewing and interpreting a culture from one's own cultural perspective.

Ethnographer: An anthropologist who spends time residing with a group of people in order to understand that way of life.

Ethnography: A written description of a group of people and their culture, as studied by an ethnographer.

Evangelists: Protestant missionaries.

Evidence: Data that can be applied to the solution of a research question or problem.

Fer-de-lance: Large poisonous snake (Bothrops asper). See **Nauhyaca**.

Field notes: Written and/or tape recorded information that is collected during the course of fieldwork.

Fieldwork: The activity of collecting information by visiting or residing in the community being studied.

Genealogy: A record of kinship relationships, through both "blood" and marriage.

Godparenthood: See **Compadrazgo.**

Holistic: Viewing all aspects of a cultural or social system; focusing on the interrelations among the parts of those systems.

Huitlacoche: An edible fungus that grows on corn cobs in the fields.

Hypothesis: An educated guess that can serve as the basis for research.

Ideal/real culture: **Ideal culture** is the "ought to" version, what the people say they "ought to do or think"; **real culture** is what they actually do or think.

Informant: A person who provides the ethnographer with information. Given the sometimes negative connotations of this term, some ethnographers call them **assistants** or **consultants**.

Interviewing: Asking direct questions of the community residents; interviews may be structured ahead of time with a particular goal in mind (e.g., gathering census data), or may be more casual and open-ended (as in gathering a life history).

Key informant: A person on whom the ethnographer relies heavily for information. A key informant may have specialized skills or knowledge, an important status in the society, or perhaps just a lot of available time.

Kiln: A large oven used for firing pottery.

Life history: A person's life-story and the context in which it has been lived.

Machete: Long, broad-bladed knife used as a tool or weapon.

Madrina: Godmother, usually sponsoring her godchild in the baptism ceremony.

Maize: Corn.

Mano: See **Metate.**

Masa: Maize dough.

Mestizo: A person of mixed native and Spanish ancestry.

Metate: A flat stone used for grinding maize kernels into a dough; used with a **mano**, or hand-sized grinding stone.

Midwife: A female curer who not only delivers babies but also is usually an expert in natural (e.g., herbal) remedies.

Milpa: A cultivated field.

Mole: A sauce made from chocolate, chiles, and various spices and seeds; usually served with turkey or chicken.

Monte: Wild, untamed, uncultivated lands.

Municipio: A governmental jurisdiction, like a county in the United States.

Nahua: People who speak the Nahuatl language and practice customs identified with this ethnic group.

Nahuatl: A native language in Mexico, spoken today by approximately 1 million people.

Nauhyaca: A poisonous snake (Bothrops asper). See **Fer-de-lance**.

Network path: An individual or institution that can facilitate your entry into your chosen community.

Nortes: Chilly winter-time winds.

Objectivity: Maintaining an unbiased attitude; not making judgments.

Olla: Tall earthenware container, usually for water or other liquids.

Otomí: A native group, neighbors of the **Nahua**.

Padrino: Godfather, usually sponsoring his godchild in the baptism ceremony.

Participant observation: A fieldwork technique whereby the ethnographer participates in the activities of the society while at the same time being a keen observer.

Pastoral: A way of life dependent primarily on the raising of herd animals.

Plaza: An open area in the center of the community; usually the site for the market, social events, and some religious rituals.

Presidente: The highest official political position in the community; like a "mayor."

Pulque: A fermented drink made from maguey (agave) syrup. Called **octli** in Nahuatl.

Quechquemitl: A triangular garment worn by native women over their blouses and usually woven on the **backstrap loom**.

Quesadillas: Flat, filled tortillas. The name implies a cheese filling, but other fillings are used as well.

Rapport: Quality of interpersonal relations; may be good or bad.

Reciprocity: Equal exchanges, usually involving goods or services rather than money. These exchanges bind people together socially and politically.

Registro de Bautismos: Record of baptisms in a church.

Registro de Matrimonios: Record of marriages in a church.

Relativism: Viewing and understanding a culture from the point of view of the members of that culture.

Role: The expectations attached to a person's status; how one is expected to carry out one's responsibilities.

San Isidro: A Catholic saint, patron of farmers.

Semilla de Culebra: Literally, "snake seed," this is a type of hibiscus. As a treatment for snakebite, chewed seeds are placed over the bite.

Shaman: A religious specialist whose main role is to cure people.

Snakestone: Usually hard concretions found in animal stomachs, but may also be kidney or bladder stones. Applied directly to a snakebite wound for healing.

Status: A person's position in a group or society (such as wife, teacher, or shaman).

Tamale: Maize dough filled with meat or fruits, and wrapped in corn husks or banana leaves. Tamalli, in Nahuatl.

Tequila: A distilled drink from the juice of the maguey (agave) plant.

Tianguiz: A native market, usually held once or twice a week in a particular community. Called Tianquiztli in Nahuatl.

Todos Santos: "All Saints" day, welcoming the souls of deceased adults. See **Day of the Dead.**

Totonac: A native group, neighbors of the Nahua.

SOME USEFUL REFERENCES

Accounts of interesting fieldwork experiences can be found in nearly every ethnography--few ethnographers can resist the temptation to include them. The *Case Studies in Cultural Anthropology* series edited by George and Louise Spindler since 1960, includes ethnographies that relate especially revealing field experiences. Particularly enlightening are:

Basso, Ellen B. 1973. *The Kalapalo Indians of Central Brazil*. Fort Worth: Harcourt Brace.

Chagnon, Napoleon. 1997. *Yanomamo*. 5th ed. Fort Worth: Harcourt Brace.

Heider, Karl. 1979. *Grand Valley Dani: Peaceful Warriors*. Fort Worth: Harcourt Brace.

Lee, Richard B. 1984. *The Dobe !Kung*. Fort Worth: Harcourt Brace.

Parman, Susan. 1990. *Scottish Crofters: a Historical Ethnography of a Celtic Village*. Fort Worth: Harcourt Brace.

A number of books are explicitly devoted to recounting anthropologists' field experiences. These include:

Anderson, Barbara Gallatin. 1990. *First Fieldwork: the Misadventures of an Anthropologist*. Prospect Heights, Ill.: Waveland Press.

Barley, Nigel. 2000. *The Innocent Anthropologist*. Prospect Heights, Ill.: Waveland Press.

Chagnon, Napoleon. 1974. *Studying the Yanomamo*. New York: Holt, Rinehart and Winston, Inc.

Chiñas, Beverly. 1993. _La Zandunga: of Fieldwork and Friendship in Southern Mexico_. Prospect Heights, Ill.: Waveland Press.

DeVita, Philip, ed. 1990. _The Humbled Anthropologist: Tales from the Pacific_. Belmont, CA.: Wadsworth Publishing Co.

DeVita, Philip, ed. 1991. _The Naked Anthropologist: Tales from Around the World_. Belmont, CA.: Wadsworth Publishing Co.

Dumont, Jean-Paul. 1978. _The Headman and I: Ambiguity and Ambivalence in the Fieldwork Experience_. Austin: University of Texas Press.

Hayano, David. 1990. _Road Through the Rain Forest_. Prospect Heights, Ill.: Waveland Press.

Lareau, Annette and Jeffrey Shultz, eds. 1996. _Journeys Through Ethnography: Realistic Accounts of Fieldwork_. Boulder, CO.: Westview Press.

Mitchell, William. 1987. _The Bamboo Fire_. Prospect Heights, Ill.: Waveland Press.

Powdermaker, Hortense. 1966. _Stranger and Friend: the Way of an Anthropologist_. New York: W.W. Norton and Company.

Rabinow, Paul. 1977. _Reflections on Fieldwork in Morocco_. Berkeley: University of California Press.

Raybeck, Douglas. 1996. _Mad Dogs, Englishmen, and the Errant Anthropologist: Fieldwork in Malaysia_. Prospect Heights, Ill.: Waveland Press.

Rynkiewich, Michael A. and James P. Spradley. 1976. _Ethics and Anthropology: Dilemmas in Fieldwork_. New York: John Wiley and Sons.

Shaffir, William B. and Robert A. Stebbens, eds. 1991. *Experiencing Fieldwork: an Inside View of Qualitative Research.* Newbury Park, CA.: Sage Publications.

Skibo, James. 1999. *Ants for Breakfast: Archaeological Adventures among the Kalinga.* Salt Lake City: University of Utah Press.

Smith, Carolyn D. and L. William Kornblum, eds. 1996. *In the Field: Readings on the Field Research Experience.* Westport, CT.: Praeger.

Vogt, Evon Z. 1994. *Fieldwork Among the Maya.* Albuquerque: University of New Mexico Press.

Beyond experiential accounts, tomes have been written about fieldwork methodologies and techniques. Some of the more thorough, useful, and accessible are:

Agar, Michael. 1996. *The Professional Stranger: an Informal Introduction to Ethnography.* San Diego: Academic Press.

Bernard, H. Russell. 1988. *Research Methods in Cultural Anthropology.* Beverly Hills, CA.: Sage Publications.

Crane, Julia G. and Michael V. Angrosino. 1992. *Field Projects in Anthropology: a Student Handbook.* Prospect Heights, Ill.: Waveland Press.

De Munck, Victor and Elisa J. Sobo. 1998. *Using Methods in the Field: A Practical Introduction and Casebook.* Walnut Creek: AltaMira Press.

Ellen, R. F., ed. 1984. *Ethnographic Research: a Guide to General Conduct.* London: Academic Press.

Emerson, Robert M., Rachel I. Fretz, and Linda L. Shaw. 1995. *Writing Ethnographic Field Notes.* Chicago: University of Chicago Press.

Fetterman, David M. 1989. *Ethnography: Step by Step*. Applied Social Research Methods Series, vol. 17. Newbury Park: Sage Publications.

Freilich, Morris. 1977. *Marginal Natives at Work: Anthropologists in the Field*. New York: John Wiley and Sons.

Kutsche, Paul. 1998. *Field Ethnography: a Manual for Doing Cultural Anthropology*. Upper Saddle River, NJ.: Prentice Hall.

Naroll, Raoul and Ronald Cohen (editors). 1973. *A Handbook of Method in Cultural Anthropology*. New York: Columbia University Press.

Pelto, Pertti J. and Gretel H. Pelto. 1978. *Anthropological Research: the Structure of Inquiry*. 2d ed.. Cambridge: Cambridge University Press.

Schensul, Stephen L., Jean J. Schensul, and Margaret D. LeCompte. 1999. *Essential Ethnographic Methods: Observations, Interviews, and Questionnaires*. Walnut Creek: Altamira Press, Vol. 1, *The Ethnographer's Toolkit*, Jean J. Schensul and Margaret D. LeCompte, eds.

Stocking, George W., Jr. 1983. *Observers Observed: Essays on Ethnographic Fieldwork*. History of Anthropology, vol. 1. Madison: University of Wisconsin Press.

Watson, C. W. (editor). 1999. *Being There: Fieldwork in Anthropology*. London: Pluto Press.

Weiss, Robert. 1994. *Learning from Strangers: the Art and Method of Qualitative Interview Studies*. New York: The Free Press.

Werner, Oswald and G. Mark Schoepfle. 1986-87. *Systematic Fieldwork*, 2 vols. Beverly Hills: Sage Publications.

Whyte, William Foote. 1984. *Learning from the Field: A Guide from Experience.* Beverly Hills: Sage.

Whyte, William Foote. 1997. *Creative Problem Solving in the Field: Reflections on a Career.* Walnut Creek: AltaMira Press.

Wolcott, Harry F. 1995. *The Art of Fieldwork.* Walnut Creek: AltaMira Press.

Also useful, for further references on fieldwork, is:

Gravel, Pierre Bettez and Robert B. Marks Ridinger. 1988. *Anthropological Fieldwork: an Annotated Bibliography.* New York: Garland Publishing, Inc.

If you are interested in the lifeways and cultures of the peoples in the general region of fictional Amopan, you may wish to consult:

Bernard, H. Russell and Jesús Salinas Pedraza. 1989. *Native Ethnography: a Mexican Indian Describes his Culture.* Newbury Park, AC.: Sage Publications.

Granberg, Wilbur J. 1970. *People of the Maguey: the Otomí Indians of Mexico.* New York: Praeger.

Montoya Briones, José de Jesús. 1964. *Atla: Etnografía de un Pueblo Nahuatl.* Mexico: Instituto Nacional de Antropología e Historia.

Reck, Gregory G. 1978. *In the Shadow of Tlaloc: Life in a Mexican Village.* Prospect Heights, Ill.: Waveland Press.

Sandstrom, Alan R. 1991. *Corn is Our Blood: Culture and Ethnic Identity in a Contemporary Aztec Indian Village.* Norman: University of Oklahoma Press.

Sandstrom, Alan R. and Pamela E. Sandstrom. 1986. *Traditional Papermaking and Paper Cult Figures of Mexico*. Norman: University of Oklahoma Press.

Schryer, Frans J. 1980. *The Rancheros of Pisaflores: the History of a Peasant Bourgeoisie in Twentieth-Century Mexico*. Toronto: University of Toronto Press.

Slade, Doren L. 1992. *Making the World Safe for Existence: Celebration of the Saints among the Sierra Nahuat of Chignautla, Mexico*. Ann Arbor: The University of Michigan Press.

Taggart, James M. 1983. *Nahuat Myth and Social Structure*. Austin: University of Texas Press.

Taggart, James M. 1997. *The Bear and His Sons: Masculinity in Spanish and Mexican Folktales*. Austin: University of Texas Press.

Williams Garcia, Roberto. 1963. *Los Tepehuas*. Xalapa, Ver.: Universidad Veracruzana Instituto de Antropología.

WORKBOOK

GETTING THERE

ANSWER FORM

Write your answers on this form. You do not need to repeat the questions.

1. _____

2. _____

3. a) _____

   b) _____

4. _____

5. _____

6. _____
   _____
   _____
   _____
   _____

7. _____
   _____
   _____

8. _____
   _____
   _____

9. _____
   _____

10. _____
    _____
    _____
    _____

FIRST ENCOUNTERS

ANSWER FORM

Write your answer on this form. You do not need to repeat the questions.

A1. _____

A2.

_____

_____

A3. _____

_____

_____

_____

_____

A4.

_____

_____

A5. _____

B1. _____

B2. _____

B3. _____

B4. _____

B5. _____

C1

    a)_____

_____

    b)_____

_____

_____

    c)_____

_____

_____

d)

C2.

C3.

C4.
a)
b)
c)
d)
e)
f)

C5.

C6.

C7.

C8.

C9.

WHO'S WHO IN AMOPAN

ANSWER FORM

Write your answers on this form. You do not need to repeat the questions.

A1.

_____
_____
_____

A2.

_____
_____
_____
_____

A3.

_____
_____
_____
_____
_____

B1.

_____
_____

B2.

_____
_____
_____
_____

B3.

_____
_____
_____
_____

C1.

_____

C2.

C3.

C4.

C5.
    a)

    b)

C6.

D1. Do this on a separate sheet of paper.

D2.

Status Rank (1=highest	Household (name of head)	Bases for Judgment
1		
2		
3		
4		
5		
6		
7		

D3. So this on the map (next page)

CENSUS OF AMOPAN - AUGUST 1965
B.E. Radcliffe - Pritchard

Res. Num.	Occupants	Relation to Household Head	Age	Gender	Marital Status	Occupation	Launguage Spoken	Other Relatives
6	Miquel Costero	Head	66	M	M	Basketmaker	Spanish + Nahuati	Francisco (brother, deceased)
	Alicia	Wife	61	F	M	Basketmaker	Nahuati	Robert (Son in Mexico City)
	Pedro	Son	42	M	W	Basketmaker Laborer	Spanish + Nahuati	Salvador (Son in Mexico City)
	David	Grandson	22	M	M	Farmer	"	Celeste (daughter, deceased)
	Gloria	Grandson's Wife	18	F	M	Housewife	"	
	Francisca	Grand daughter	19	F	Engaged To Sam Pescadero	Help at home	"	Marta (daughter, married, in Clintan)
	Maria	Grand daughter	18	F	S	Help at home	"	

59

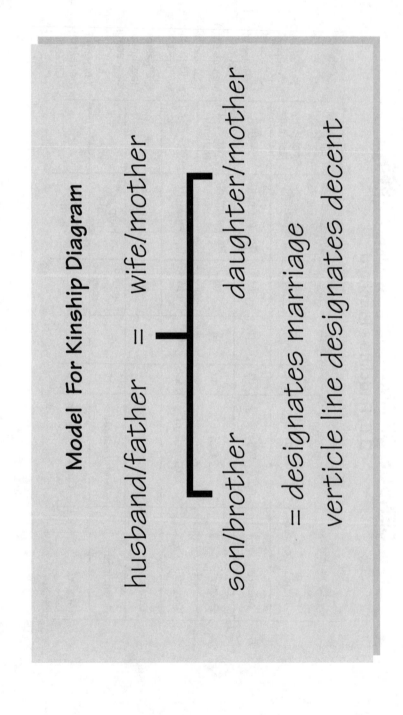

Model For Kinship Diagram

husband/father = wife/mother

son/brother   daughter/mother

= designates marriage
verticle line designates decent

60

CENSUS FORMS

Residence #	Occupants	Relation to Household head	Age	Gender	Marital Status	Occupation	Language Spoken	Other Relatives

CENSUS FORMS

Residence #	Occupants	Relation to Household head	Age	Gender	Marital Status	Occupation	Language Spoken	Other Relatives

CENSUS FORMS

Residence #	Occupants	Relation to Household head	Age	Gender	Marital Status	Occupation	Language Spoken	Other Relatives

MAP OF AMOPAN

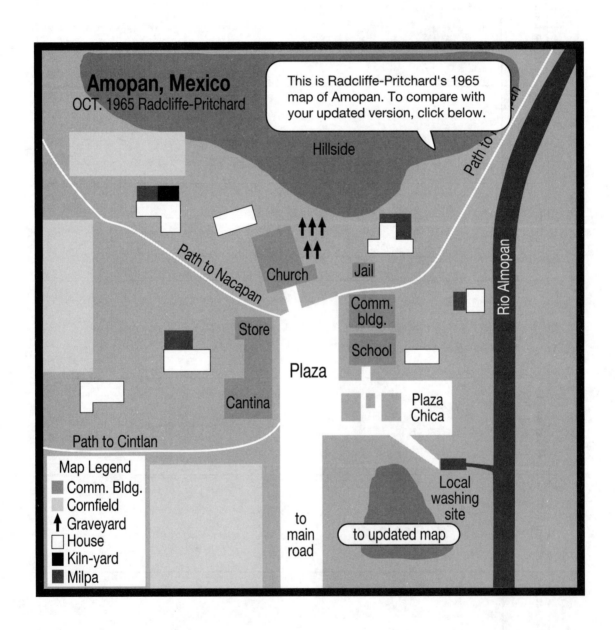

WORKING IN THE FIELDS

ANSWER FORM

Write your answers on this form. You do not need to repeat the questions.

A1.

_____

_____

_____

_____

A2.

_____

_____

A3.

_____

_____

_____

_____

B1.

1)_____

2)_____

3)_____

_____

_____

_____

B2.

_____

B3.

_____

B4.

_____

B5.

_____
_____
_____
_____

C1.

_____
_____
_____

C2.

_____
_____
_____
_____

D1.

_____
_____

D2.

_____
_____
_____

D3.

_____
_____

D4.

_____
_____
_____

D5.

D6.

D7.

D8.

WORKING IN THE FIELDS: CULTIVATION DATA

Juan Milpero and Eduardo Jefe have given you plenty of information on the agricultural cycle (schedule) for the major Amopan crops. Enter this information on the table below.

Crop	Prepare Field	Plant	Weed	Harvest
White maize				
Yellow maize				
Black beans				
Garbanzos				
Melons				
Green chiles				
Sugar cane				

MARKETDAY

ANSWER FORM

A1.

_____
_____
_____
_____

A2.

_____
_____
_____
_____

A3.

_____
_____

A4.

_____

A5.

_____
_____
_____

A6.

_____
_____

A7.

_____
_____

A8.

_____
_____

A9.

_____
_____

A10.

_____
_____
_____

B1.

_____
_____
_____

B2.

_____
_____
_____
_____

C1. Use attached table and diagram.

MARKETDAY: INFORMATION ON MARKET VENDORS

Complete the following table about market vendors and their commodities. The stall numbers on this table correspond to the numbers on the accompanying diagram.

Stall #	Type of Commodity	Specific Products	Name of vendor (if known)	Place where goods produced	Other (e.g., pricing, quality)
1					
2					
3					
4					
5					
6					
7					
8					
9					
10					
11					
12					
13					
14					
15					
16					
17					
18					
19					
20					
21					
22					
23					

DIAGRAM OF AMOPAN'S MARKET

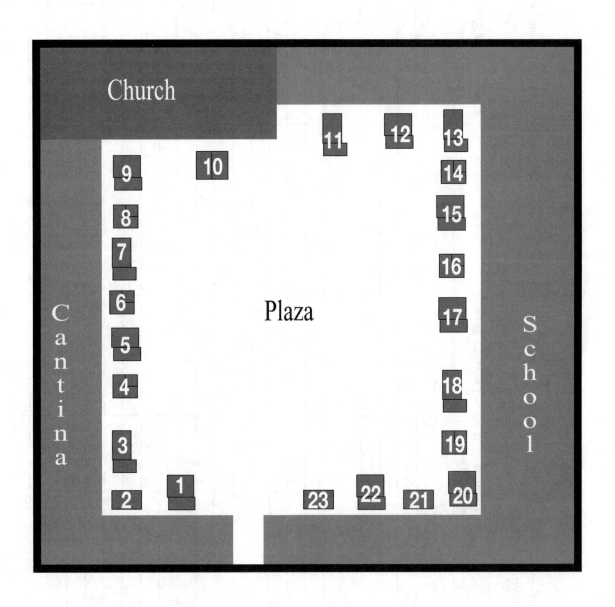

THE DAY OF THE DEAD

ANSWER FORM

Write your answers on this form. You do not need to repeat the questions.

A1.

        a) _____

        b) _____

        c) _____

        d) _____

        e) _____

        f) _____

        g) _____

        h) _____

_____

_____

A2.

        a) _____

_____

        b) _____

_____

        c) _____

_____

        d) _____

_____

A3.

_____

_____

B1.

    a)_____

    b)_____

    c)_____

    d)_____

    e)_____

B2.

_____
_____
_____

B3.

_____
_____
_____
_____
_____

C1.

_____
_____
_____
_____

C2.

_____
_____

    a)_____

    b)_____

    c)_____

THE DAY OF THE DEAD

COMPARATIVE INTERVIEW RESPONSES

Question #	Milpero response	Pescadero response	Jefe response
1			
2			
3			
4			
5			
6			
7			
8			
9			
10			
11			
12			

Question #	Milpero response	Pescadero response	Jefe response
13			
14			
15			

FIELDNOTES

FIELDNOTES

FIELDNOTES

FIELDNOTES

SINGLE PC LICENSE AGREEMENT AND LIMITED WARRANTY